JOHN JACOBSON'S
Silly Songs & Sing-Alongs for Composers
NEW LYRICS TO OLD FAVORITES

TABLE OF CONTENTS

HAL•LEONARD®
CORPORATION
7777 W. BLUEMOUND RD. P.O. BOX 13819 MILWAUKEE, WI 53213

Visit Hal Leonard Online at
www.halleonard.com

Bach, the Great Composer

(to the tune of "London Bridge")

Arranged with New Lyrics by JOHN JACOBSON
Piano Accompaniment by DEAN CROCKER

Für Beethoven
(to the tune of "Für Elise")

Arranged with New Lyrics by JOHN JACOBSON
Piano Accompaniment by DEAN CROCKER

6

Brahms
(to the tune of "When Irish Eyes Are Smiling")

Arranged with New Lyrics by JOHN JACOBSON
Piano Accompaniment by DEAN CROCKER

3/13

Handel, Handel
(to the tune of "Sailing, Sailing")

New Words and Arrangement by JOHN JACOBSON
Piano Accompaniment by DEAN CROCKER

Lively (♩. = 108)

Piano

Hook elbows with the people in your row.

The entire row sways L

Han - del, Han - del played on the harp - si -
Han - del, Han - del wrote things that we could

chord,_____ and dab - bled up - on the or - gan ev'ry -
sing,_____ like op - er - a, and a - ri - a and

Bow to neighbor on one side then the other

With a partner, do the Minuet or Hesitation Waltz, holding upstage hands.
Step together   *Apart*   *Together*

Han - del, Han - del wrote or - a - to - ri -

Apart   *Together*   *Apart*

os,_____ can - ta - tas, tri - os, op - 'ras and the

Together   *Apart*   *Let go of partner, and wag R index finger at audience*

or - gan con - cer - to._____ Han - del's

H-A-Y-D-N
(to the tune of "BINGO")

Arranged with New Lyrics by JOHN JACOBSON
Piano Accompaniment by DEAN CROCKER

Oh, Where Have You Been, Mendelssohn?

(to the tune of "Billy Boy")

Arranged with New Lyrics by JOHN JACOBSON
Piano Accompaniment by DEAN CROCKER

7/17

Amadeus Mozart, What Can I Say?
(to the tune of "Skip to My Lou")

New Words and Arrangement by JOHN JACOBSON
Piano Accompaniment by DEAN CROCKER

Lively (♩ = 108)

Snap fingers twice — *Shrug* — *Snap twice* — *Shrug*

A-ma-de-us Mo-zart, what can I say? A-ma-de-us Mo-zart, what can I say?

Snap twice — *Shrug* — *Pretend to play keyboard ... crossing hands, then open, and repeat*

A-ma-de-us Mo-zart, what can I say? Played an a-maz-ing cla - vier.

Churn Choo Choo arms, once per measure

Op - er - a and or-ches-tra, cham-ber mu - sic, sym-pho-ny; writ-ing mu - sic

26

Johann Strauss
(to the tune of "Oh, My Darling, Clementine")

New Words and Arrangement by JOHN JACOBSON
Piano Accompaniment by DEAN CROCKER

With anticipation (♩ = 132)

Stand by with hands behind back

1st time: Hitchhike twice R   *Hitchhike twice L*

2nd Time: March 6 steps

If you trav-eled to Vi-en-na back in
Man-y march-es, plen-ty pol-kas and a

1st time: Hitchike twice R   *Twice L*   *Wave as in "hello"*

2nd time: Hands over head with fingers together   *Wipe a la "safe"*

eight-een for-ty-two,   you might meet a man named Jo-hann who could
bal-let. What a thrill! When he was-n't writ-ing waltz-es, he com-

Silly Songs & Sing-Alongs for Composers – Teacher Edition

30

Igor Stravinsky
(to the tune of "Wait for the Wagon")

New Words and Arrangement by JOHN JACOBSON
Piano Accompaniment by DEAN CROCKER

32

This Is a Verdi Day!

(to the tune of "La Donna è Mobile")

New Words and Arrangement by JOHN JACOBSON
Piano Accompaniment by DEAN CROCKER

36

Reproducible Pages

Lyric Sheets

Composer Biographies

Composer Activities

Lyric Sheet

Bach, the Great Composer

(to the tune of "London Bridge")
New Lyrics by John Jacobson

Oh, Johann Sebastian Bach,
J.S. Bach, J.S. Bach.
Oh, Johann Sebastian Bach,
Great composer!

Born in sixteen eighty-five,
eighty-five, eighty-five.
Born in sixteen eighty-five,
Great composer!

He was born in Eisenach,
Eisenach, Eisenach.
He was born in Eisenach,
Great composer!

Bach wrote many symphonies,
Sonatas, cantatas.
Penned a few partitas,
Great composer!

He liked to play the harpsichord,
Organ too, and clavichord.
And he played the violin,
Great composer!

J.S. Bach went for "Baroque,"
for "Baroque," for "Baroque."
J.S. Bach went for "Baroque,"
Great composer!

J.S. Bach had twenty kids,
twenty kids, twenty kids.
J.S. Bach had twenty kids,
Great composer!

Für Beethoven

(to the tune of "Für Elise")
New Lyrics by John Jacobson

Once there was a man named Beethoven,
Who wrote a piece called "Für Elise."
He was born in Bonn, that's Germany
In Seventeen and Seventy.

He could really play the piano
And violin under his chin.
Some called him a child prodigy,
That means he's good as kids can be.

He was the king of counterpoint,
And not a note would disappoint.
But he couldn't hear a thing!

So he wrote a lot of string quartets,
And even penned some minuets.
And he wrote a lot of symphonies,
Not all of these were "Für Elise."

Now if you like an opera,
You ought to know *Fidelio*.
This guy wrote a lot of notes!

Once there was a man named Beethoven,
Who wrote a piece, called "Für Elise."
He's the greatest writer of them all.
We give a "ten" to Beethoven!

Brahms

**(to the tune of
"When Irish Eyes Are Smiling")
New Lyrics by John Jacobson**

Johannes Brahms was born
Back in eighteen thirty-three.
Makes him twice as old as grandpa;
Forty times as old as me!

He was a true romantic
Of the purest German kind,
But he had trouble sleeping.
He had so much on his mind.

With Bach and Ludwig Beethoven,
He was third of the awesome "B's,"
But each night, he tossed and tumbled,
As he dreamed up symphonies.

He played the horn and cello;
Laid awake and thought of them.
Then he took up piano,
And wrote "German Requiem."

It's hard to go on writing,
When you can't getting any sleep.
So Brahms spent many hours
Just sadly counting sheep!

Johannes Brahms is smiling,
And if you should wonder why,
Oh, he fin'lly fell asleep
To his perfect lullaby.

Handel, Handel

**(to the tune of "Sailing, Sailing")
New Lyrics by John Jacobson**

Handel, Handel
Played on the harpsichord,
And dabbled upon the organ
Everyday that he was bored.
Handel, Handel
Worked for the British king.
He loved composing music
More than any other thing.

Handel, Handel
Wrote things that we could sing,
Like opera and aria and lots of other things.
He did Baroque just like composer Bach.
Between the two of them,
They made the German churches rock!

Handel, Handel
Wrote oratorios,
Cantatas, trios, operas
And the organ concerto.
Handel's father
Urged him to study law,
But Handel got a handle
And he wrote "Hallelujah!"

OK TO REPRODUCE

H-A-Y-D-N

(to the tune of "BINGO")
New Lyrics by John Jacobson

There was a dude in Austria
And Haydn was his name! Oh,
H A Y D N, H A Y D N,
H A Y D N,
And Haydn was his name.

His parents knew he had a gift,
So shipped him off at six. Oh,
(clap) A Y D N, *(clap)* A Y D N,
(clap) A Y D N,
And Haydn was his name.

He learned to play the harpsichord
And the violin! Oh,
(2 claps) Y D N, *(2 claps)* Y D N,
(2 claps) Y D N,
And Haydn was his name.

So he went to Vienna
To sing in the boys choir.
(3 claps) D N, *(3 claps)* D N,
(3 claps) D N,
And Haydn was his name.

He taught Ludwig van Beethoven,
And he knew Mozart too. Oh,
(4 claps) N, *(4 claps)* N,
(4 claps) N,
And Haydn was his name.

The Father of the string quartet
And of the symphony. Oh,
(5 claps) *(5 claps)* *(5 claps)*
And Haydn was his name.

Oh, Where Have You Been, Mendelssohn?

(to the tune of "Billy Boy")
New Lyrics by John Jacobson

Oh, where have you been, Mendelssohn, Mendelssohn?
Oh, where have you been, great composer?
"I am writing symphonies, for it is my expertise!"
You're a genius and very fine conductor.

Oh, where are you from, Mendelssohn, Mendelssohn?
Oh, where are you from, great composer?
"Born in eighteen hundred nine,
Somewhere near the river Rhine."
You're a genius and very fine conductor.

Can you play the organ, too, Mendelssohn, Mendelssohn?
Can you play the organ, too, great composer?
"I can play the organ, too,
And it's what I like to do."
You're a genius and very fine conductor.

Is that oratorio, Mendelssohn, Mendelssohn?
Is that oratorio, great composer?
"If you really want to know,
I do oratorio!"
You're a genius and very fine conductor.

Did you meet a famous queen, Mendelssohn, Mendelssohn?
Did you meet a famous queen, great composer?
"Yes, I met Victoria;
She liked my work *Elijah!*"
You're a genius and very fine conductor.

Are you writing something new, Mendelssohn, Mendelssohn?
Are you writing something new, great composer?
"Sure, I'm writing up in heaven;
Died in eighteen forty-seven."
You're a genius and very fine conductor!

Amadeus Mozart, What Can I Say?

(to the tune of "Skip to My Lou")
New Lyrics by John Jacobson

Amadeus Mozart, what can I say?
Amadeus Mozart, what can I say?
Amadeus Mozart, what can I say?
Played an amazing clavier.

Opera and orchestra,
Chamber music, symphony;
Writing music people sang,
All with a name like Wolfgang!

Mozart makes you want to dance.
Mozart makes you want to prance.
Come along and take a chance,
Dance with a man named Mozart.

And we'll be dancing with Amadeus.
We'll minuet or do a silly jig.
And when we're dancing with Amadeus,
We'll all look great in powdered wigs!
(spoken) Hooray!

Amadeus Mozart, what can I say?
Amadeus Mozart, what can I say?
Amadeus Mozart, what can I say?
Played an amazing clavier.

Johann Strauss

(to the tune of "Oh, My Darling, Clementine")
New Lyrics by John Jacobson

If you traveled to Vienna
Back in eighteen forty-two,
You might meet a man named Johann
Who could write a note or two.

He's the Waltz King!
He's the Waltz King,
Writing music full of schmaltz!
But we love him; please more of him.
We salute you, Johann Strauss!

Many marches, plenty polkas
And a ballet. What a thrill!
When he wasn't writing waltzes,
He composed a cool quadrille!

He's the Waltz King!
He's the Waltz King,
Writing music full of schmaltz!
But we love him; please more of him.
We salute you, Johann Strauss!

Though he's gone now, really gone now,
You can find him on the tube.
If you listen very closely,
You might hear the "Blue Danube."

He's the Waltz King!
He's the Waltz King,
Writing music full of schmaltz!
But we love him; please more of him.
We salute you, Johann Strauss!

OK TO REPRODUCE

Lyric Sheet

Igor Stravinsky

(to the tune of "Wait for the Wagon")
New Lyrics by John Jacobson

When I was just a toddler sitting on my father's knee,
He told me of a writer by the name of Stravinsky!

Igor Stravinsky! Igor Stravinsky!
Igor Stravinsky wrote some pretty "out there" stuff!

Oh, he was born in Russia back in eighteen eighty-two,
But ended up in Hollywood, as many people do.

Igor Stravinsky! Igor Stravinsky!
Igor Stravinsky wrote some pretty "out there" stuff!

He played around with rhythm
And he tried most any thing,
Especially in a ballet that he called the "Rite of Spring."

Igor Stravinsky! Igor Stravinsky!
Igor Stravinsky wrote some pretty "out there" stuff!

Now some may say his music sounds really quite absurd,
But nothing's more exciting than to hear his "Firebird!"

("Firebird" excerpt)

Igor Stravinsky! Igor Stravinsky!
Igor Stravinsky wrote some "out there" stuff!
I can't get enough!
I guess you can see, I like Stravinsky!

This Is a Verdi Day!

(to the tune of "La Donna è Mobile")
New Lyrics by John Jacobson

This is a Verdi Day,
Giuseppe Verdi Day!
A time for all to play;
A special holiday.

Three cheers and hip hoorah!
Let's sing some opera.
We could do "Nabucco"
Or "Rigolet(eh)to!"

Sing Italiano,
Loud or più piano.
We could do "Aida" or
"Il trovatore!"

Tra la la, tra la la, tra la la la la la la la lee.
Tra la la, tra la la. Sing along with Verdi!

If you should ever go
To visit Milano,
You'll hear them sing and play
A very Verdi way.

Hear the soprano float.
He gave her lots of notes.
In a pizzeria, *(pih-zah-ree-ah)*
You'll hear his aria. *(ah-ree-ah)*

None as good as Verdi,
'cept perhaps Puccini, *(poo-chee-nee)*
Singing at La Scala, *(Scah-lah)*
An aria for you.

Tra la la, tra la la, tra la la la la la la la lee.
Tra la la, tra la la. Sing along with Verdi!

OK TO
REPRODUCE

Johann Sebastian Bach

Born: Eisenach, Germany 1685
Died: Leipzig, Germany 1750

Johann Sebastian Bach was one of the greatest composers of all time. He wrote a lot of music! In fact, he wrote more than 1,100 pieces in almost every genre of music you can imagine, except opera. In addition to being a composer, he was an organist, a violinist and a teacher.

Bach lived in Germany. He came from a family of musicians. His father was one, too. Not only did he write a lot of music, he also had a lot of children – twenty, to be exact! He had to compose a lot of music just to keep food on the table for all those hungry mouths. Four of his children went on to become famous musicians in their own right.

Bach is often considered the King of Baroque music. The word Baroque comes from the Italian word *barocco*, which means bizarre. There really is nothing bizarre about Bach's music, but describing it as Baroque indicates it is exciting, exuberant, orderly and just plain brilliant!

Bach's music was not widely known during his life. In fact, it wasn't until about a hundred years after his death that he was rediscovered and his genius finally recognized. Since then, most will agree that he is one of the best there ever was.

Did I mention he had a lot of children?

What have you learned about Bach through song and story?
Fill in the blanks with your answers.

1. Bach was born in

   _____ Germany.

2. Name three of the instruments Bach played.

   _____

   _____

3. _____ of Bach's twenty children became famous musicians.

4. Bach wrote during the _____ Period in music history.

OK TO
REPRODUCE

Ludwig van Beethoven

Born: Bonn, Germany   1770
Died: Vienna, Austria   1827

Can you imagine being one of the greatest composers of all time and not being able to hear your own music? Well, that is what happened to the one and only Ludwig van Beethoven. You see, by the time he was grown up and successful as a composer and a conductor, he had lost almost all of his hearing. He could only imagine what his music sounded like, yet he wrote some of the most beautiful music ever composed.

Beethoven's father was his first music teacher, so that gave him quite a headstart. His father really thought that Ludwig could be the next child prodigy like Mozart, so he had him out performing for the public at a very early age. He played the piano, the organ, the violin and the viola. Believe it or not, he even got to have a music lesson from Mozart himself and with another famous composer, Franz Joseph Haydn. All that training certainly paid off because by the time he was a teenager, Beethoven already had published his first compositions and people were starting to compare him to the great Mozart. Having a good music teacher is obviously very important to anyone's education!

Beethoven was born in Bonn, Germany but spent most of his adult years in Vienna, Austria. He wrote an astonishing amount of music: nine symphonies, an opera, many concertos, and so much more.

Beethoven is thought of as the bridge between the Classical and the Romantic styles of music,

and most would agree that no single composer in the history of humankind had a more profound influence on music than Ludwig van Beethoven. Sadly, as an adult, he never heard a note of it!

What have you learned about Beethoven through song and story?
Fill in the blanks with your answers.

1. Beethoven's first music teacher was

   _____. (his father)

2. By the time Beethoven was an adult,

   he was losing his _____,

   but he continued to compose music

3. One of Beethoven's most famous

   symphonies is _____ _____

4. Beethoven was _____ years old when
   he died.

Johannes Brahms

Born: Hamburg, Germany   1833
Died: Vienna, Austria   1897

When people talk about the three Bs of musical composition, you can bet they are talking about Beethoven, Bach and none other than Johannes Brahms.

Just mention the Romantic period of music, and the first name that often comes to mind is Johannes Brahms. Like Beethoven, Brahms was born in Germany, but spent most of his professional life in Vienna, Austria.

It's interesting that many composers, like J.S. Bach for instance, were not very famous as composers while they were alive. That is not the case with Johannes Brahms. Lots of people knew him and he was very successful and well respected even while he was alive.

Also like Beethoven, Brahms's father was a musician and his first teacher. When Brahms was seven years old, his father handed him off to a better piano teacher. By age ten, he was playing public concerts.

Brahms started composing music fairly early in his life, but he wasn't very happy with many of the results. Believe it or not, he took it upon himself to destroy most of those early works. Lucky for us, his later works survived and are some of the finest examples of the music of the Romantic period.

What have you learned about Brahms through song and story?
Fill in the blanks with your answers.

1. Who are the 3 "B's" of musical composition?

    _____

    _____

    _____

2. What 2 instruments did Brahms play the best?

    _____

    _____

3. (T or F) Brahms was well known as a composer while he was alive.

4. Why did Brahms destroy most of his early compositions?

    _____

5. Brahms wrote during the _____ Period in music history.

Silly Songs & Sing-Alongs for Composers – Teacher Edition

Composer Bio

Georg Frideric Handel

Born: Halle, Germany   1685
Died: London, England   1759

When people in churches or at shopping malls stop everything they are doing and sing "Hallelujah!" at the top of their lungs, they are singing the triumphant music of Georg Frideric Handel. This "Hallelujah" chorus is from a large choral work called *Messiah*. It's an oratorio and is Handel's most famous piece of music. It may be only a legend, but it is sometimes said that when the choir first performed the "Hallelujah" chorus for the king of England, he was so moved that he rose to his feet to honor it. Now, more than 250 years later, it is tradition that when we sing or listen to this fantastic work, we all stand up and revel in it as well. It is amazing how music can move us, even across the generations!

Of course, Georg Frideric Handel wrote and played a lot of other music, too. He was a very accomplished player of the harpsichord and the pipe organ. Believe it or not, his father wanted him to be a lawyer and not a musician, so Handel had to practice secretly on a small clavichord smuggled into the attic. Good thing for us, he did!

Handel was lucky to live and study in Germany, Italy and England. All of those marvelous experiences are reflected in his music. Besides *Messiah*, Handel wrote 30 other oratorios (choral dramas), 42 operas, more than 120 cantatas, trios and duets—not to mention arias, chamber music, odes, serenatas and 17 organ concerti. That's a lot of notes, and when you put them all together, they represent the work of one of the finest composers of the Baroque period, Georg Frideric Handel.

What have you learned about Handel through song and story?
Fill in the blanks with your answers.

1. Name two instruments Handel played.

   _____

   _____

2. Handel's father wanted him to be a

   _____, not a musician.

3. What tradition began over 250 years ago when we sing "The Hallelujah Chorus"?

   _____

4. Name 4 different types of music Handel wrote.

   _____

   _____

   _____

   _____

OK TO REPRODUCE

Franz Joseph Haydn

Born: Rohrau, Austria   1732
Died: Vienna, Austria   1809

When Franz Joseph Haydn was only six years old, his parents sent him off to a neighboring town to study music. You see, even though they both loved him and music very much, they knew he would never get the kind of training he deserved in their poor little town. Haydn never again returned to live with his parents.

When Haydn was eight, he was singing in his beautiful soprano voice when he was "discovered" and taken off to Vienna to sing with the famous Vienna Boys Choir for nine years.

While he was in Vienna, young Joseph studied Latin and other school subjects, but also voice, violin and keyboard. However, he did not receive much training in the "mechanics" of music like theory and counterpoint. It wasn't until he was a young adult that he was able to study these very important skills, but it wasn't long before he matured into one of the most accomplished composers of the Classical period.

Ludwig van Beethoven studied composition with Haydn in Vienna. So, it seems very clear that Haydn had significant influence over classical and romantic styles of music.

Franz Joseph Haydn was described as an honest and humble man with a great sense of humor for practical jokes that can sometimes even be found in his music.

Joker or not, Haydn is often referred to as the "Father of the Symphony" for the important contributions he made to that art form. Others suggest that "Father of the String Quartet" would be even more appropriate because, when it comes to that form of music, there is none better than Franz Joseph Haydn.

What have you learned about Haydn through song and story?
Fill in the blanks with your answers.

1. Haydn left home at the age of _____ to study music.

2. Haydn was "discovered" at the age of 8 and asked to sing with the famous

   _____ _____ _____,

   which he did for _____ years.

3. While in London, one of Haydn's students was _____.

4 Haydn was also known as the Father of the _____ and the

   _____ _____.

Felix Mendelssohn

Born: Hamburg, Germany   1809
Died: Leipzig, Germany   1847

Besides having a lot of names, Jakob Ludwig Felix Mendelssohn–Bartholdy had a lot of talents. As a German composer writing in the Romantic period, he was also very well regarded as a pianist, organist and conductor.

One of the greatest contributions Mendelssohn made was to reintroduce the world to the music of his predecessor, Johann Sebastian Bach. Remember that while Bach was alive, his music was not well known. Thanks to Mendelssohn, there was a revival of interest in Bach's music, which made him an important figure in the history of music.

Indeed, Mendelssohn did so much more. First a child prodigy in his lifetime, he went on to write many symphonies, concerti, oratorios, and much piano and chamber music. His musical compositions were greatly influenced by composers such as Bach, Handel and Mozart.

One sad aspect of Mendelssohn's life was the prejudice that was levied toward him because of his Jewish faith. This prejudice continued even after Mendelssohn was no longer alive! Eventually, times changed and now he is very highly regarded as one of the finest composers of the Romantic era.

What have you learned about Mendelssohn through song and story?
Fill in the blanks with your answers.

1. One of Mendelssohn's greatest contributions was reviving an interest in the musical works of _____.

2. Besides a composer, Mendelssohn was also a fine pianist, organist and _____.

3. Mendelssohn studied and loved the music of _____, _____, and _____.

4. Queen Victoria especially liked Mendelssohn's work entitled _____.

5. Mendelssohn was regarded as one of the finest composers of the _____ era.

OK TO REPRODUCE

Wolfgang Amadeus Mozart

Born: Salzburg, Austria   1756
Died: Vienna, Austria   1791

Look closely at the dates above and you will notice that Wolfgang Amadeus Mozart lived a very short life. He died when he was only 35 years old! Yet in those very short years, he managed to become one of the greatest composers of all time, writing more than 600 works!

Mozart was a child prodigy and composer in the classical style. He wrote everything from symphonies, to concertos, chamber music, piano and choral pieces and even opera.

Wolfgang spent his early years in Salzburg, Austria and was so good at the keyboard and the violin that he was traveling all over Europe performing for kings and queens by the time he was only five years old. At the age of twelve, Mozart wrote his first opera!

Discontent with what small-town Salzburg had to offer, by his mid-twenties Mozart had settled in Vienna, the world's great capital of music. He spent most of his short adult life there. He became famous, but at times could hardly make a living!

Though Mozart was quite a jokester, as a musician and composer, there may have been none better. In fact, composer Joseph Haydn once said of Mozart, "Posterity will not see such a talent again in 100 years." Some might even say "ever."

What have you learned about Mozart through song and story?
Fill in the blanks with your answers.

1. Mozart was a child _____,

   and was performing for kings and queens

   at the age of _____, and had written

   his first opera when he was _____.

2. Mozart played an amazing

   _____.

3. Mozart composed a large variety of

   musical compositions, including music

   people could sing and _____ to.

4. Mozart died at the age of _____.

5. Despite his short life span, he wrote over

   _____ musical works!

OK TO REPRODUCE

Composer Bio

Johann Strauss II

Born: Vienna, Austria   1825
Died: Vienna, Austria   1899

If you do your homework, you will discover that there are several members of the extended Strauss family that did very well in the area of musical composition. Richard Strauss (1864-1949) was a leading German composer of the Romantic period. Johann Strauss I was quite a well-known composer of dance music. The composer we celebrate in this silly song today is the son of Johann Strauss I. We know him well as Johann Strauss II, or Johann Strauss Jr, or "the Waltz King."

Why "the Waltz King," you might ask? The waltz is a dance in three-quarter time (beats grouped in 3) that became all the rage in Vienna back in the 19th century. That popularity was mostly due to the efforts of our Johann Strauss II.

Even though Johann's father was a composer, this was not the life he had in mind for his son. In fact, he envisioned him a banker, but banking was not in the stars for Johann II, so he defied his father and went on to study music. Eventually, he surpassed even his father as a musician and as a composer. This did not go very real well with Papa Strauss and they maintained a musical rivalry throughout the elder's life. When Johann I died, our Waltz King had the stage all to himself. He toured Austria, Poland and Germany with his orchestra. He even conducted in the United States.

One of Strauss' most famous waltzes is entitled "The Blue Danube." It is so beautiful that when the famous composer Johannes Brahms heard it

for the first time, he scribbled a note full of playful envy under the title. The note read, "Unfortunately, *not* by Johannes Brahms." It is clear that Brahms recognized the King of the Waltz as well.

What have you learned about Strauss through song and story?
Fill in the blanks with your answers.

1. Father Strauss wanted his son to be a

   _____.

2. The _____ is a dance with _____ beats to a measure that became very popular in Vienna back in the 19th century.

3. (T or F) Johann Strauss the First was known at the Waltz King?

4. (T or F) Strauss I and II had a close father-son relationship.

5. "The _____ _____"
   is one of Strauss' most famous waltzes.

Igor Stravinsky

Born: Lomonosov, Russia   1882
Died: New York City, USA   1971

Not all the composers we sing about in this silly song collection lived during the Baroque, Classical or Romantic period, nor were all of them German or Italian. Igor Stravinsky was born in Russia, moved to France and eventually became a naturalized American living in California and then New York City until his death in 1971.

Stravinsky is often considered one of the most influential composers of the twentieth century. If you ever get a chance to listen to and see his ballets "Firebird" or "The Rite of Spring," you will understand why.

Stravinsky was known as a composer who liked to break all the rules and try new things with music. As a result, much his music caused a lot of conversation and even some controversy. He experimented with sounds and rhythms that often shocked audiences. However, breaking musical rules is often necessary to push the art form forward and create something new and exciting. Stravinsky did this regularly.

One time, Stravinsky went so far as to change a chord in "The Star Spangled Banner." This was in Boston in 1944. He was threatened with a fine and told that it was against the law to rearrange the National Anthem. It is not the first or the last time someone would almost be arrested for playing music!

Throughout his life, Stravinsky continued to bend and break the rules of what people thought of as proper musical composition. Because of his courage and vision, the rules of music are often seen in a new light. When that happens, something very special can often emerge … like spring … like a firebird … like Stravinsky!

> **What have you learned about Stravinsky through song and story?**
> *Fill in the blanks with your answers.*
>
> 1. Stravinsky was born in _____;
>   he kept moving westward and eventually
>   became a citizen of _____.
>
> 2. Stravinsky wrote music that experimented
>   with crazy _____ and _____
>   that often times shocked audiences.
>
> 3. Two of his famous ballets were
>   "_____" and "The Rite of Spring."
>
> 4. (T or F) One time, Stravinsky tried to change
>   a chord in "America, the Beautiful."

Composer Bio

Giuseppe Verdi

Born: Roncole, Italy   1813
Died: Milan, Italy   1901

If you've ever gone to see an opera, there is a very good chance that you have heard the music of Giuseppe Verdi. Opera was what Verdi became very famous for and the world is better because of it.

Verdi was an Italian composer who wrote during the Romantic period. He didn't just compose operas, but they are certainly his most famous and lasting works of art. *Nabucco, Rigoletto, Aida, La Traviata, Macbeth,* and *Falstaff* are Verdi operas and the list goes on and on.

When Verdi was born, the part of Italy his family lived in was actually part of France, but Verdi is all Italian. In his twenties, Verdi moved to Milan to continue his studies. He studied theory and counterpoint and everything that it takes to be a great composer. He wrote his first opera at the age of twenty-six and went on to produce many operas for La Scala, the opera house in Milan. To this day, La Scala is a center of the opera world, to a great extent because of Verdi's writings.

When Verdi died in 1901, much of the country turned out for his funeral. It remains one of the largest public gatherings in the history of Italy. You might say he had a funeral of opera-size proportions.

What have you learned about Bach through song and story?
Fill in the blanks with your answers.

1. Verdi was from the country of

    _____ and he most famous

    for writing _____.

2. Name 3 of Verdi's operas.

    _____

    _____

    _____

3. The famous opera house in Milan is called

    _____

4. What is the largest public gathering in the

    history of Italy? _____

    In what year did it happen? _____

Name _____ Class _____

Composer Word Search

DIRECTIONS: Locate and circle these 20 words in the word search puzzle.
They can go forward, backward, in a straight line or diagonally.

```
D  U  O  M  U  Y  G  S  R  U  I  M  S  F  Z  Y  C  M  P  Y  O  U  K  H  J
Q  R  D  E  C  O  X  L  B  L  Y  K  T  M  X  A  I  I  F  J  M  H  V  G  Y
P  S  O  H  I  K  J  Z  K  L  R  Z  R  R  E  U  M  Z  P  Z  M  D  Z  F  M
Z  O  X  M  A  W  N  D  M  R  U  M  A  J  I  N  B  Y  X  V  E  R  D  I  E
J  X  N  B  A  Y  P  U  P  P  Q  C  V  K  K  Y  D  E  Q  P  U  L  U  O  G
V  N  J  W  D  N  D  I  J  E  C  O  I  T  S  T  K  E  S  B  V  K  N  P  J
J  I  B  W  K  A  T  N  A  A  U  M  N  Z  T  C  B  K  L  D  C  W  B  G  V
E  Y  O  A  S  S  Y  I  V  N  L  P  S  H  R  C  L  A  S  S  I  C  A  L  C
H  B  W  L  R  U  T  B  C  V  O  O  K  Q  A  U  G  S  Y  D  S  C  A  K  W
T  R  R  K  I  O  H  E  J  O  L  S  Y  L  U  V  B  E  E  T  H  O  V  E  N
J  A  N  G  I  N  Q  A  L  T  M  E  J  X  S  E  I  U  D  J  Z  H  H  D  Q
A  H  B  S  E  L  U  U  N  T  V  R  Q  L  S  A  S  N  H  H  X  C  Z  N  H
U  M  S  W  A  L  T  Z  E  D  L  R  G  E  S  Y  M  P  H  O  N  Y  N  E  Z
T  S  S  F  X  Q  O  O  Z  L  E  Y  M  O  Z  A  R  T  C  V  P  O  A  Q  B
Z  C  O  O  N  U  O  U  G  X  B  L  W  P  T  A  B  A  C  H  F  Z  S  A  F
I  W  W  D  S  T  K  X  L  C  R  O  R  G  E  D  S  S  T  F  K  V  F  V  D
S  M  C  O  N  C  E  R  T  O  O  P  E  R  A  M  W  X  O  D  H  A  H  D  F
```

Verdi	Bach	Handel	Mozart	Beethoven	Mendelssohn
Strauss	Brahms	Stravinsky	Haydn	Baroque	Romantic
Classical	Composer	Opera	Waltz	Symphony	Piano
Violin	Concerto				

Composer Activity

Name _____ Class _____

Composer Fun Facts Puzzle

DIRECTIONS: Complete this crossword puzzle from the clues below about the ten composers we have just studied.

Across

3. destroyed most of his early works
5. his music caused controversy
8. dance in three-quarter time
12. famous ballet by Stravinsky
13. a practical joker
14. Queen Victoria's favorite
16. sang with the Vienna Boys Choir
17. Brahms' "_____ Requiem"
18. home of La Scala
19. Waltz King
22. lost most of his hearing
23. only lived 35 years

Down

1. revived the music of Bach
2. Beethoven's "Für _____"
4. Handel's most famous piece of work
6. famous for writing operas
7. famous Strauss waltz, "The Blue _____"
9. Bach's hometown
10. Handel played this instrument when he was bored
11. a very musical child
15. Mozart's first name
20. Bach had ___ children
21. "Hallelujah Chorus" tradition
22. King of Baroque

Silly Songs & Sing-Alongs for Composers – Teacher Edition

Page 43
1. Eisenach
2. organ, violin, harpsichord, clavichord
3. 4
4. Baroque

Page 44
1. his father
2. hearing
3. Für Elise
4. 57

Page 45
1. Bach, Beethoven, Brahms
2. horn and cello
3. T
4. he didn't think they were very good
5. Romantic

Page 46
1. harpsichord, pipe organ
2. lawyer
3. everyone stands
4. oratorios, operas, cantatas, trios and duets, arias, chamber music, odes, serenatas, and organ concerti

Page 47
1. 6
2. Vienna Boys Choir; 9
3. Beethoven
4. Symphony; String Quartet

Page 48
1. Bach
2. conductor
3. Bach, Beethoven, Mozart
4. Elijah
5. Romantic

Page 49
1. prodigy; 5; 12
2. clavier
3. dance
4. 35
5. 600

Page 50
1. banker
2. waltz; 3
3. F
4. F
5. Blue Danube

Page 51
1. Russia; America
2. sounds; rhythms
3. Firebird
4. F

Page 52
1. Italy; operas
2. Nabucco, Rigoletto, Aida, La Traviata, Macbeth, Falstaff
3. La Scala
4. Verdi's funeral; 1901

Page 53

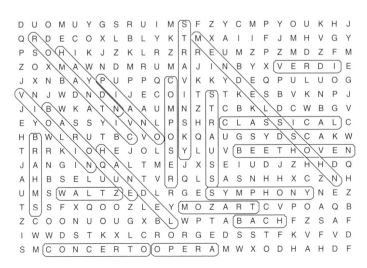

Page 54

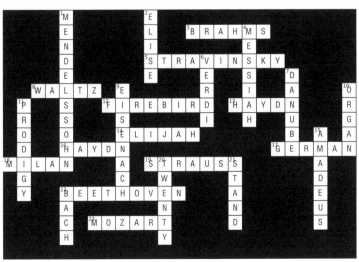

About the Writer

John Jacobson

In October of 2001 President George Bush named **JOHN JACOBSON** a *Point of Light* award winner for his "dedication to providing young people involved in the arts opportunities to combine music, charitable giving and community service." John is the founder and volunteer president of *America Sings!* Inc., a non-profit organization that encourages young performers to use their time and talents for community service. With a bachelor's degree in Music Education from the University of Wisconsin-Madison and a Master's Degree in Liberal Studies from Georgetown University, John is recognized internationally as a creative and motivating speaker for teachers and students involved in choral music education. He is the author and composer of many musicals and choral works that have been performed by millions of children worldwide, as well as educational videos and tapes that have helped music educators excel in their individual teaching arenas, all published exclusively by Hal Leonard Corporation. John has staged hundreds of huge music festival ensembles in his association with Walt Disney Productions and directed productions featuring thousands of young singers including NBC's national broadcast of the Macy's Thanksgiving Day Parade, presidential inaugurations and more. John stars in children's musical and exercise videotapes, including the series *Jjump! A Fitness Program for Children* and is the Senior Contributing Writer for *John Jacobson's Music Express*, an educational magazine for young children published by Hal Leonard Corporation. Most recently, John has become a YouTube sensation and is known by millions as the "Double Dream Hands Guy!"